NATIONAL
GEOGRAPH

MW00697822

Feeding the World

Peter Winkler

PICTURE CREDITS
Cover: Kenneth Garrett/NGS Image Collection. Pages 1, 4-5 (top), 7 (low right), 12-13 (center), 20 (left), 28, 30 PhotoDisc®; pages 2–3 © Stephen St. John/NGS Image Collection; pages 4–5 © John Paul Kay/Peter Arnold, Inc.; pages 6–7, 18–19 (top) © Robb Kendrick/Aurora; page 7 (center) Robert Becker/Lincoln Journal Star/AP; page 8 (left) courtesy Bob Sakata; page 8 (right), 16 (top right) Equator Graphics; pages 8–9 © Antony Edwards/The Image Bank; page 10 Seth Perlman/AP; pages 10–11 John Colwell/Grant Heilman Photography, Inc.; page 12 Andy Sacks/Stone; page 13 Bruce Hands/Stone; page 14 (top left) Arthur C. Smith III/Grant Heilman Photography, Inc.; pages 14–15 (top) Grant Heilman/Grant Heilman Photography, Inc.; pages 14–15 © Kevin Horan/Stone; page 15 courtesy Peter Winkler; page 16 (low right) © Lowell Georgia/CORBIS; pages 16–17, 18–19 (bottom right) ISAAA; pages 18 (low left), 24 Jane Grushow/Grant Heilman Photography, Inc.; pages 20–21 (top) © Chris Rogers/Rainbow; page 20–21 (low left) © Still Pictures/Peter Arnold, Inc.; page 21 (low right) Sam Abell/NGS Image Collection; page 22 © Jeff Greenberg/Rainbow; pages 22–23 Liaison; pages 24–29 (borders) © Artville®; page 25 (top) courtesy Karen Thompson; pages 25 (low), 26, 27, 29 © Michael Newman/PhotoEdit.

Back cover: (top to bottom) © Artville®, PhotoDisc®, © Corbis Stock Market, Keith Kapple/SuperStock, Inc., PhotoDisc®.

Neither the publisher nor the author shall be liable for any damage that may be caused or sustained or result from conducting any of the activities in this book without specifically following instructions, undertaking the activities without proper supervision, or failing to comply with the cautions contained in the book.

Cover photo: People at a market in Saqqara, Egypt

Produced through the worldwide resources of the National Geographic Society, John M. Fahey, Jr., President and Chief Executive Officer; Gilbert M. Grosvenor, Chairman of the Board; Nina D. Hoffman, Executive Vice President and President, Books and School Publishing.

PREPARED BY NATIONAL GEOGRAPHIC SCHOOL PUBLISHING
Ericka Markman, Senior Vice President; Steve Mico, Editorial Director; Barbara Seeber, Editorial Manager; Lynda McMurray, Amy Sarver, Project Editors; Jim Hiscott, Design Manager; Karen Thompson, Art Director; Kristin Hanneman, Illustrations Manager; Diana Bourdrez, Stephanie Henke, Diana Leskovac, Anne Whittle, Photo Editors; Christine Higgins, Photo Coordinator; Matt Wascavage, Manager of Publishing Services; Sean Philpotts, Production Coordinator.

Production: Clifton M. Brown III, Manufacturing and Quality Control.

CONSULTANT/REVIEWER
Dr. James Shymansky, E. Desmond Lee Professor of Science Education, University of Missouri-St. Louis

PROGRAM DEVELOPMENT
Kate Boehm Jerome

BOOK DESIGN
Herman Adler Design

Published by the National Geographic Society
Washington, D.C. 20036-4688

ISBN: 0-7922-8871-8

Printed in Canada

11 10 09 08
10 9 8 7 6 5

Contents

Table

Four new babies—hungry and thirsty—are born every second. Earth has six billion people today and may have ten billion by 2050. Can we feed them all?

The question is simple, but the answer isn't. Part of the problem is money. Some people have enough to buy food. Others don't. Part of the problem is politics. Some countries work hard to feed their people. Others don't. Part of the problem is organization and transportation. Sometimes food gets to those who need it. Other times it doesn't.

In this book, we'll look at the scientific issues that arise from feeding a hungry world. Biologists, chemists, and other experts are exploring new ways to grow more food. Their research has led to big discoveries—and big questions.

Children at a food kitchen in Bangladesh

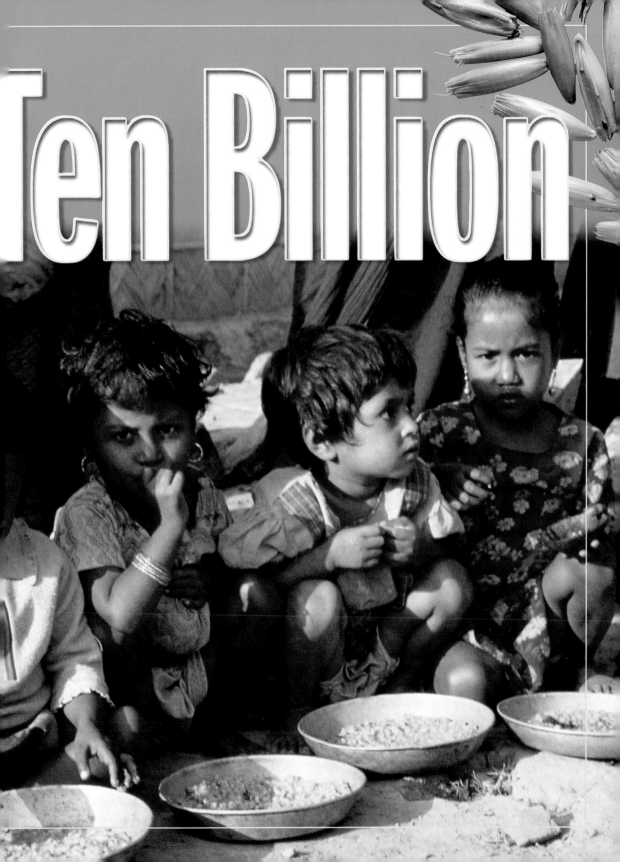

Ten Billion

A farmer in Madagascar harvests rice.

How Well Are We Doing?

Good News

- Humans produce more food than ever before. If it were divided equally, everyone would have enough.

- There are only about half as many underfed people today as there were in 1970.

- Better seeds, machines, fertilizers, and pesticides have hugely increased the amount of food farmers can grow.

Bad News

- Every day roughly 800 million people don't get enough to eat. About 200 million are hungry children.

- Some farmers can't afford the new seeds, machines, and chemicals that create larger crops.

- Modern farming, like any new way of doing things, may pose risks to human health and the environment.

- Farmers and other food producers must consider the benefits and costs of new technologies.

A farmer in Nebraska fills a truck with corn.

Science Helps Farmers Grow More Food

This Farm Is a Factory

CANADA

COLORADO UNITED STATES

PACIFIC OCEAN MEXICO

Bob Sakata

Bob Sakata says he runs a "small family farm." But his business is really more like a factory. And like most factories, the Sakata farm keeps trying to increase production.

Bob Sakata moved to Colorado in 1945 and started farming. He worked 40 acres of land. Today he and his family own 3,500 acres, on which they grow onions, cabbage, and corn. Each year Sakata sells 60 million pounds of food that later appears in supermarkets across the United States. He'd like to raise even more.

"The only way you can stay in business as a farmer is to boost your **yield** [the amount grown] and reduce your costs," says Sakata. And that's exactly what he does. In 1945 Sakata produced 200 sacks of onions per acre. Today he harvests 800 sacks from the same amount of land.

Fields of cabbage (green) and corn

High Tech, High Cost

How do science and technology help farmers like Bob Sakata raise more food? One important way is by inventing new machines that are better and faster than the old ones. For example, Sakata owns two giant machines that pick corn. The machines gently pluck each ear from the stalk and then bundle the ears together. Each machine can pick 240,000 ears of corn in a single day.

Modern farm machinery is amazing, but so is its cost. The price tag for just one of Sakata's corn-pickers is $160,000. Then there's the fuel to run the machines. And don't forget repairs. Fixing a single flat tire can cost nearly $1,000. High-tech machines can be a great help to farmers—if they can afford the high cost.

The giant tires used on some farm vehicles are very expensive.

This farm machine cuts down corn plants and harvests the ears.

A farmer adds pesticides to a tank.

Green Science

Bob Sakata and other modern farmers also get help
from biologists and chemists. Scientists have created
plants that grow faster and produce more food. Some
of these varieties produce better onions or sweeter corn.
Some can withstand colder winters or warmer summers.

Scientists have also developed powerful **fertilizers** to
help plants grow. At the same time, **pesticides** can
protect crops from insects and other enemies. These
innovations have helped humans raise more food
than ever before.

A helicopter sprays pesticides on apple trees to protect them from disease.

Red Alert?

Modern farming raises big crops—and big questions. Environmentalists warn that today's Americans use a lot of chemicals. Farmers, lawn-care companies, and backyard gardeners rely heavily on pesticides to protect their plants.

Problems arise when chemicals meant to kill pests hurt or kill other animals too. One pesticide that was used to fight gypsy moths also destroyed harmless butterflies. Another pesticide killed about 20,000 hawks.

Machines called combines harvest wheat.

Contour farming—following the land's natural shape when plowing—conserves soil.

Wind and water can erode farmland.

What happens if those same poisons seep into our food and water? That depends on the chemicals. Some might not hurt humans at all. Others may.

Farmers also face the challenge of keeping their land healthy. Earlier generations plowed vast areas, which sometimes led to **erosion**, or the wearing away of soil. Today farmers like Sakata use a variety of techniques to protect the soil. Among other things, they leave plant roots—which help to hold the soil in place—in the field.

Key Points

- New machines and chemicals help modern farmers raise huge amounts of food.

- Today's farmers have to spend lots of money if they want the latest machines and chemicals.

- Chemicals sometimes used by farmers may pose risks to human health and the environment.

CAUTION
PESTICIDE APPLICATION
KEEP   OFF

Old MacDonald

By moving genes from one living thing to another, scientists can create stronger kinds of plants. Some people think this new technology might end world hunger. Others argue that it's a recipe for disaster.

Scientist Florence Wambugu works with farmers in Kenya, a country in East Africa. She helps them grow bigger and better crops. Wambugu is especially interested in finding simple ways to raise more food.

In the past ten years, Wambugu has spent much of her time studying sweet potatoes, which are an important food in her part of Kenya. A **virus** kept attacking the plants. It stopped the sweet potatoes from growing properly. Some farmers, says Wambugu, lost three-quarters of their crops because of the virus.

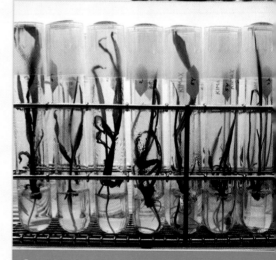

Genetically engineered corn plants in test tubes

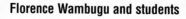

Florence Wambugu and students

A farmer plows a field in Kenya.

These healthy sweet potatoes show no signs of virus.

A sweet potato breeder checks plants in Kenya.

Designer Genes

Wambugu went to war against the virus. Her search for a weapon that could save the sweet potatoes led to a laboratory in St. Louis, Missouri. Scientists there are studying new ways to create better plants.

The lab's work focuses on **genes**, the chemical "computer programs" found in the cells of living things. Genes tell a plant to produce pink flowers or an animal to grow black hair. Now scientists have found ways to move genes from one living thing to another. That process is called **genetic engineering.**

Wambugu spent three years at the lab. Using the techniques of genetic engineering, she created a sweet potato plant that could actually fight off the virus. Wambugu tested her research in Kenya, and her plants produced magnificent sweet potatoes.

That's just the beginning, Wambugu believes. **Genetically modified foods,** she argues, could help farmers in poor countries grow desperately needed crops. "What farmers need," Wambugu says, "is technology that is packaged in the seed." No expensive chemicals, no complicated machines—just create strong plants that farmers can raise simply, and fewer people will go hungry.

Cool Science, Hot Topics

Scientists sharply disagree about genetically modified food. Supporters point to the rigorous testing of any new plant variety. They argue that high-tech foods are a safe way to improve agriculture. Some experts point out that genetically modified corn and soybeans have been widely used in the United States since 1996. They say no one has suffered as a result.

Critics warn that it's dangerous to put genes into species where they don't belong. Because genes tell the cells in plants or animals how to grow, some scientists argue that we cannot know for sure how the mixing of genes will affect plants or animals in the long term. With that in mind, many people worry about the safety of genetically modified foods.

Stay Tuned! Next time you rummage in the kitchen for a snack, take a few minutes to look at the label on your food. You can find out its ingredients, how many calories it has, and more. But you probably won't find out if any of the ingredients include genes from other species. The U.S. doesn't require food producers to label genetically modified foods. In contrast, many European countries do require such labels. Should the U.S. and other nations follow Europe's example? That's likely to be a global issue in the next few years, so stay tuned to the news.

Protesters call for labels on genetically modified foods.

Some countries require labels on genetically modified foods.

DEMAND
...ELING

DR. FRANKENFOOD

Are these foods genetically modified?
Without a label you can't tell.

California
TOMAT...
PUREE
...E WITH GENETIC...
...ODIFIED TOMATO...

...TC...
...EE

...TICALLY
...ATOES

...UBLE CONCENT...

How does eating genetically modified food affect people? No one knows for sure. Food labels in the United States don't say whether genetic engineers changed any ingredients. That makes it hard, some scientists point out, to tell if the foods are causing problems. And genetically modified foods are still fairly new. So we won't know their long-term effects for years.

Key Points

● Scientists have found ways to move genes from one living thing to another. This process is called genetic engineering.

● Genetic engineers can create plants that resist disease and fight pests. Some say that these plants could help in the struggle to feed Earth's growing population.

● Since genetically modified foods are fairly new, no one knows their long-term effects. Scientists sharply disagree about the safety of such foods.

Food kitchens in the United States provide meals for hungry people.

A boy receives a meal at a refugee camp.

Interesting Questions

How much food does a person need?

An average adult needs between 2,200 and 2,900 calories each day. Of course, no one is truly average. People who don't get much exercise need fewer calories, and active people need more. But all people require a variety of vitamins, minerals, and other nutrients to stay healthy.

What parts of the world suffer most from hunger?

According to the United Nations, Asia has the largest number of underfed people—about half a billion. Africa comes next with about 200,000,000 hungry people.

How common are genetically modified foods?

Some sources estimate two-thirds of the food items in an average U.S. supermarket contain genetically modified ingredients.

A Growing Opinion

Important issues are sometimes complicated. Yet we often face decisions about these issues, even in our everyday lives. How do we know we are making good choices? One way is to develop an informed opinion. An informed opinion is a person's thoughts, feelings, or beliefs—supported by facts—about an issue. Follow the steps and the story to find out how you can develop an informed opinion.

STEP 1 Define the Issue

Be sure you understand the issue clearly. An issue is often a question that you have to answer. Write down the issue and your choices, or the different ways that you could answer the question.

TOMATO
— Homestead —

An Excellent Salad Variety!

Seeds of Thought

Ryan and Maria need to raise money for a band trip. They decide to raise the money by growing and selling vegetables.

The two friends buy seeds and tell their green-thumbed neighbor, Mrs. Norton, about their plan. She wants to help and gives them two dozen tomato plants— and a heavy jar marked Pests-B-Gone.

"Now this," she explains, "is my secret weapon."

"Is that stuff safe?" Ryan asks.

"Sure!" Mrs. Norton replies. "Just don't let it touch your skin or eyes. Wash the veggies well before you eat them. Oh, and try not to breathe much while you're spraying."

"I don't know," says Ryan as he and Maria walk home. "We learned in school that pesticides can be bad for the environment."

STEP 2 Get the Facts

After defining the issue, you need to get the facts. When you collect the facts about an issue, get your information from the best sources you can find. You could get good facts from up-to-date library books, in respected magazines, on websites, and by asking experts.

Answers Take Root

Ryan and Maria decide they need more information before making up their minds. They spend an afternoon at the library; then they talk to experts at the local garden center. A few days later, they compare notes at lunch.

"One big problem with pesticides," says Ryan, "is that the soil absorbs the poisonous chemicals. They could seep into our drinking water."

Maria smiles. "Don't forget that there are other things we can try. The lady at the garden center suggested we buy some praying mantis eggs. When they hatch, the insects could eat some of our pests— without damaging the environment. And we could buy ladybugs, which also eat pests."

Now that the two friends know more about their choices, they're closer to a decision.

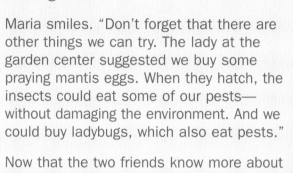

STEP 3 Evaluate the Facts

Once you've collected your information, you can evaluate your facts. One way you can do this is by making a chart. The chart can show the pros and cons, or the good and bad things, about each choice.

Which Bloom Is Better?

"We're getting way too into this, Ryan. I can't believe we're making a chart on your computer."

Ryan shrugs. "It can help us sort things out."

Pests-B-Gone	Natural Weapons
Pros	**Pros**
• Free (gift from Mrs. N.)	• Better for environment
• Mrs. N. says it really works	• No weekly spraying
	• Recommended by garden center
Cons	
• Need to spray and mix each week	**Cons**
• Danger to skin and eyes	• Need to spend money
• Could get into water supply	• Less powerful than Pests-B-Gone?

STEP 4 Form an Opinion

Think carefully about the facts you've collected and evaluated. Which choice is best supported by your facts? Does it seem like the right choice for you? If so, you have an informed opinion.

The Plan Blossoms

Looking over their chart, Ryan and Maria develop an informed opinion. "Although Mrs. Norton uses Pests-B-Gone," they agree, "let's first try Earth-friendly ways to fight pests." So the two friends head back to the garden center for ladybugs and praying mantis eggs.

The questions Ryan and Maria faced give you a small taste of the complex science that goes into your food. Do you agree with the choice the two friends made? How would you develop an informed opinion about this issue?

Farmers, scientists, environmentalists, and government leaders don't always agree on the best ways to produce food. But almost everyone agrees on one thing: It takes careful research, hard thought, and creative imagination to feed our growing world.

Food for Thought

Have a Byte

Alliance for Better Foods
www.betterfoods.org
Hear from supporters of genetically modified food.

Bob Sakata Interview
www.sb2000.com/sakata-words.html
The veteran farmer discusses his work.

Center for Food Safety
http://www.centerforfoodsafety.org/
Hear from critics of genetically modified food.

EPA: Pesticides and Food
www.epa.gov/pesticides/food
The Environmental Protection Agency provides information for families.

Sticky Rice

Genetic engineers and their opponents are clashing bitterly over "golden rice," a new variety that includes daffodil genes. The grain was designed to help people get more Vitamin A. That's important, because Vitamin A helps prevent blindness. And in some areas of the world, many kids lose their vision each year.

Some people think genetically modified rice is a great way to help children in poor countries. The company that helped create golden rice plans to donate seeds to poor farmers. Could anyone argue against that?

Yes, they could. Opponents of golden rice argue that kids would have to eat 20, 30, 40, or even more bowls daily to get enough Vitamin A. Critics say big companies are using kids to draw attention away from the dangers of genetically modified food.

You can learn more about the golden rice controversy at *www.biotech-info.net/golden.html*.

Glossary

erosion (*ee–ROH–shun*) – process in which wind or water carries soil away

fertilizer (*FUR–tuh–lie–zuhr*) – substance (often manure or chemicals) added to soil so that plants will grow better

gene – chemicals in the cells of a living thing that tell it how to grow

genetic engineering – process by which genes are moved from one living thing to another to introduce desired characteristics

genetically modified food (*juh–NET–ik–uh–lee MOD–ih–fyed FOOD*) – food item to which scientists have added genes from a different living thing

pesticide (*PES–tuh–side*) – poison used to kill insects and other organisms that eat or damage crops

virus (*VY–ruhs*) – very small particle that can destroy cells and cause disease when it grows inside plant and animal cells

yield – the amount of something, such as a crop, that is produced

Index